Bethea verDorn

Day Breaks

Illustrated by Thomas Graham

Arcade Publishing | New York

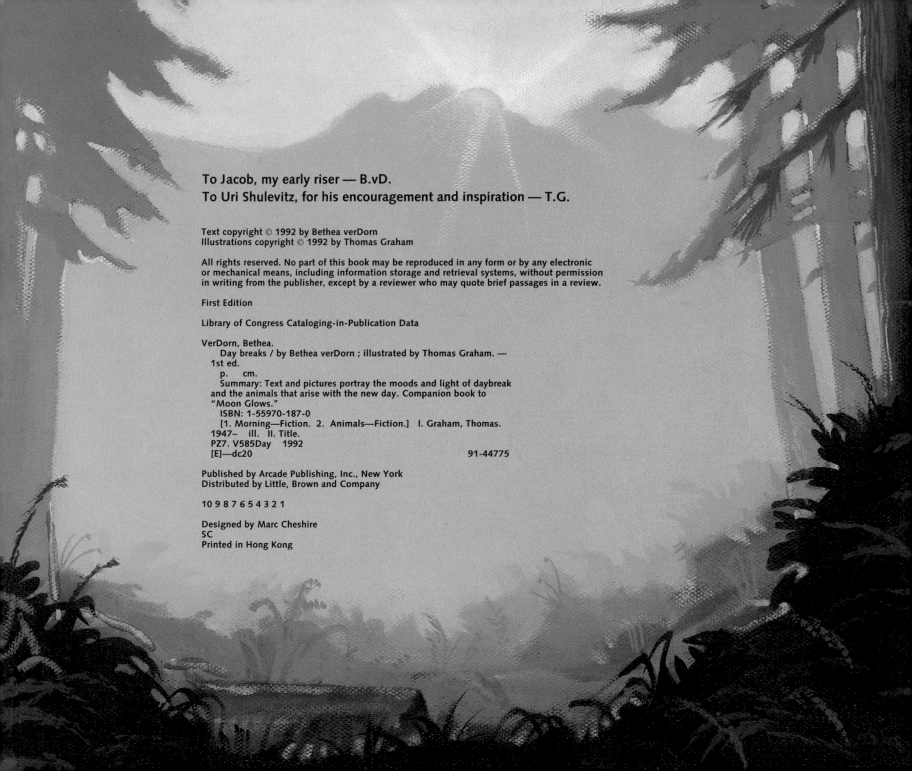

To Jacob, my early riser — B.vD.
To Uri Shulevitz, for his encouragement and inspiration — T.G.

Text copyright © 1992 by Bethea verDorn
Illustrations copyright © 1992 by Thomas Graham

First Edition

Library of Congress Cataloging-in-Publication Data

VerDorn, Bethea.
    Day breaks / by Bethea verDorn ; illustrated by Thomas Graham. —
1st ed.
    p.   cm.
    Summary: Text and pictures portray the moods and light of daybreak
and the animals that arise with the new day. Companion book to
"Moon Glows."
    ISBN: 1-55970-187-0
    [1. Morning—Fiction. 2. Animals—Fiction.]   I. Graham, Thomas.
1947–   ill. II. Title.
PZ7. V585Day   1992
[E]—dc20   91-44775

Published by Arcade Publishing, Inc., New York
Distributed by Little, Brown and Company

10 9 8 7 6 5 4 3 2 1

Designed by Marc Cheshire
SC
Printed in Hong Kong

Day breaks, and forest stirs in the morning mist.
Ferns glisten with dew. Pines push to the sky.

Deer scamper out to the meadow!

Day breaks, and canyon echoes with morning calls.
Rocks turn into rainbows at the dawn's first light.

Eagle soars to her nest!

Day breaks, and market bustles with its morning load of apples and oranges, tomatoes and corn.

Kittens pounce and purr!

Day breaks, and ocean crashes with the morning tide.
Swimmers stroll the beach. Sailboats suddenly appear.

Sea lion takes a dive!

Day breaks, and river ripples in the morning rain.
Fishermen watch for some sign of a catch.

Frog leaps to snatch a fly!

Day breaks, and desert whispers in the morning sun.
Temperature rises. Cactus bristles and blooms.

Lizard darts into the shade!

Day breaks, and cornfield rustles with the morning breeze.
Scarecrow nods and waves. Tractor plows a row.

Rooster wakes his brood!

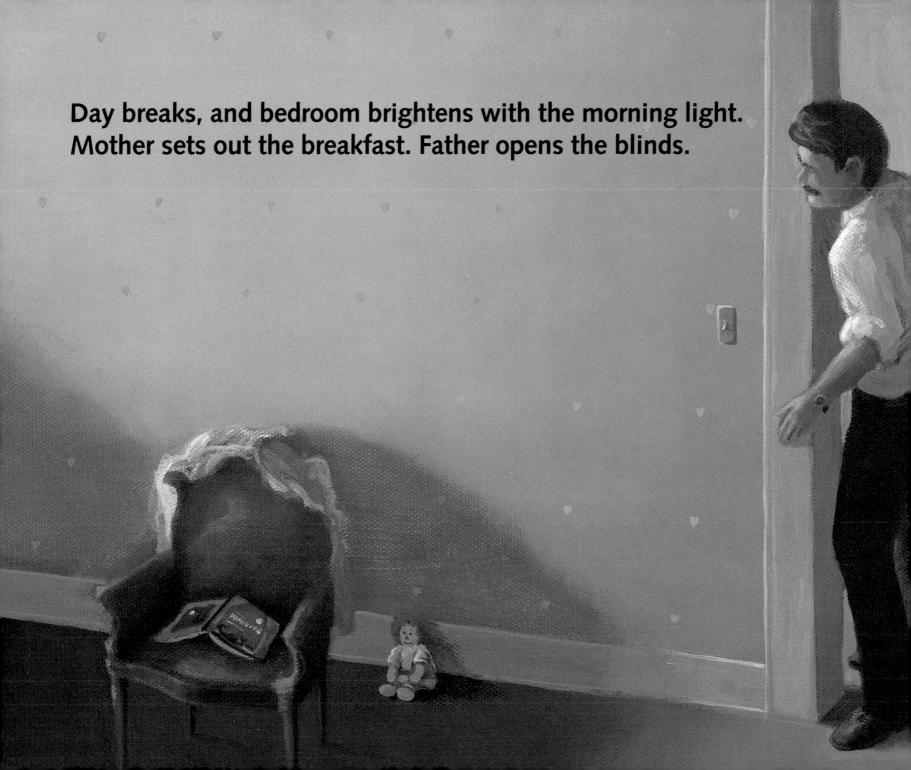

Day breaks, and bedroom brightens with the morning light.
Mother sets out the breakfast. Father opens the blinds.